HOW DO YOU DEAF?

Kerry Tidman

for Zendaya

May you always know who you are,
even when the world tries
to make you forget.
You are my why, my light,
and my reminder that
our voices matter.
This is for you - and every time
I stayed quiet so you never have to.

Dear Reader,

Before you turn the first page, I want to say something gently but clearly:

You don't need to have it all figured out.
This isn't a test.
There are no grades.
There's no one way to be deaf, or to be **you**.

This book is a space, a safe one.
A place where you can think, feel, explore, unlearn, and come home to yourself.

I wrote **'How Do You Deaf?'** for those people, like me, who never quite saw themselves in books.
For the ones who were told they were "too much", "too quiet", "too sensitive" — or "not deaf enough".

For those who masked, mimicked, and tried so hard to be "normal", they forgot what it felt like to just **be.**

So, before you begin, take a breath.
Find a comfy corner.
Make your favourite drink.
Grab a pen, a journal, some colours or just your open heart.

This book is part story, part reflection, part healing ritual.

At the end of each chapter, you'll find gentle prompts - little questions to help you meet yourself with kindness.
You can write down your thoughts.
Doodle. Scribble. Bullet-point.
Sit with them in stillness.
There is no right way. Just *your* way.

You might feel things as you read.
Anger. Sadness. Pride. Joy. Confusion. Peace.
Let it all be welcome. Let it move through.
And if it ever feels heavy, pause.
Take a break. Talk to someone safe. Come back when you're ready.

Healing isn't a race. It's a return.
A remembering.
A rebuilding.
A reclamation of all the parts of you that deserve to be seen.

If nothing else, let this book remind you:

- **You are not broken.**
- **You are not too late.**
- **You are not alone.**

This is your invitation to rise.
To soften.
To reconnect.
To be deaf on *your* terms.
To be *you* - fully, bravely, unapologetically.

I'm so honoured you're here.

With warmth, strength, and gold,

Kerry

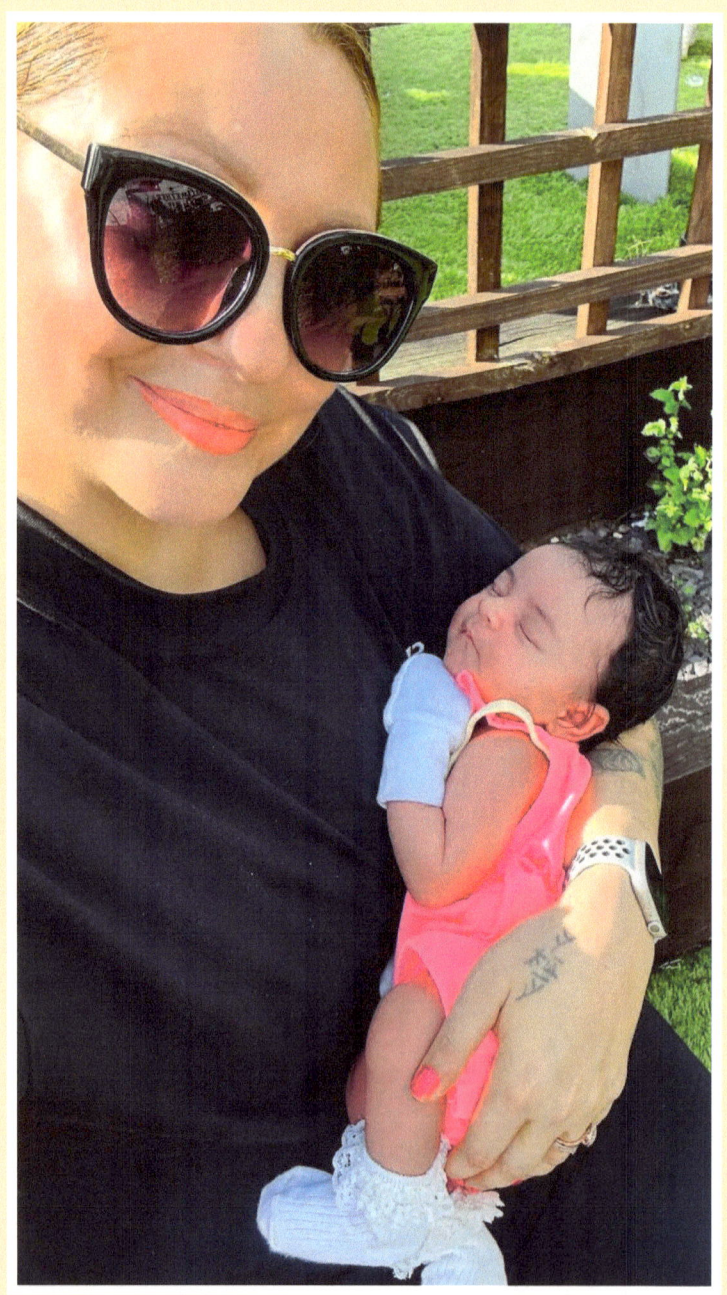

Chapter One

THERE'S NO BOOK FOR THIS

A few years ago, I became a grandma.
I was still young. Still figuring out life in many ways.
But when I held my granddaughter for the first time, something shifted.
In her tiny face, I saw a new chapter begin.
Not just for my daughter… but for me, too.

We had been in the hospital for three days.
Three days of emotion, adrenaline, strength, and surrender.
I watched my daughter, the same girl I'd raised through chaos and calm, bring new life
into the world.

And in the middle of it all, she looked at me and said:

"Mum… how do you do this? How do you be a parent?"

I smiled through the tears. My heart full and aching all at once.
And I said something I truly believed:

"There's no book for this. No rules. You just do the best you can with the version of you that exists at the time."

She nodded. And life carried on. But that moment stayed with me.
It echoed louder than I expected.
Because later that night, as the hospital buzzed around us and the world outside stayed still,
I thought about what I'd said, and who I was when I said it.

I wasn't just thinking about motherhood.
I was thinking about deafness.
About identity.
About the parts of me I had buried, and the ones I was still trying to reclaim.

There's no book for this.
No manual on how to navigate the world when you don't quite fit in.
No perfect guide to being deaf, or hard of hearing, or in between.
No clear path for what it means to grow up
feeling like too much, and not enough, all at once.

But in that moment, I realised something:

If I wanted this little girl to grow up loving who she is, I'd have to show her what that looked like.

Not in words. But in how I lived.
How I owned my story.
How I claimed my identity — fully, freely,
without apology.

I wanted her to see her grandma as bold, proud, deaf, and **thriving.**

And for that to happen, I had to become the version of me I had once needed.

That moment didn't just make me a grandma.
It made me a mirror, a legacy in motion.

And that was the beginning.
Not just of her life, but of **mine, all over again.**

Reflective prompt

- If someone younger than you asked how to love themselves, what would you say?

- What's one part of yourself you want to embrace more fully — starting today?

Space for reflection

Chapter Two
SAYING IT OUT LOUD

"I'm deaf."

It's only three words.
But for the longest time, I couldn't say them, not really.
Not with certainty. Not without shame.

I didn't grow up claiming that word.
In fact, I avoided it.
Because the world around me had already decided what being "deaf" was supposed to look like —
and I didn't fit the picture.

I could speak.
I wore hearing aids.
I passed for hearing, most of the time.

So instead, I floated in this strange in-between.

Too deaf to be hearing.
Too hearing to be "deaf enough".
And I stayed there, quietly wondering if I belonged anywhere at all.

Then the pandemic hit.
And everything changed.

Overnight, the whole world was wearing masks.
And I couldn't lipread anymore.

Suddenly, all the silent work I'd done to blend in, to guess my way through conversations, to smile and nod at the right moments —
it wasn't enough.

I was struggling.
Exhausted.
Everyday tasks became battles.
The supermarket, the chemist, the school run, everything took more energy than I had.

And then one day, at the checkout… I cracked.

The cashier spoke. I couldn't understand her.
I tried to guess. Tried to smile it off.
But inside, I was crumbling.

And the words came out.
Raw. Blurted. Unfiltered.

"I'm deaf."

Not softly. Not confidently.

They came out wrapped in frustration, tangled in embarrassment.

Because part of me still felt like I was doing something wrong.
Like I was failing at being "normal".
Like I was still waiting for someone to tell me it was okay to own that word.

That night, I went home and said it again.
To my husband. To my kids.

"I'm actually deaf."

And as soon as I said it…
I realised I had been holding my breath for years.

All this time, I had been waiting for permission.
Permission to claim it.
To stop explaining.
To stop apologising.
To just… be.

That moment — standing in the supermarket, mask between us, voice trembling —
it changed something.

I didn't feel confident yet.
But I felt real.
And sometimes, that's where all healing begins.

Reflective prompt

- Have you ever felt like you didn't belong in a certain identity or community?

- What words do you hesitate to say about yourself — and why?

- Who told you that you couldn't claim who you are? Were they right?

Space for reflection

Chapter Three

THE THINGS THEY TOLD ME

Deafness is a hidden disability.
That means most people don't see it, and when they don't see it, they make assumptions.

Growing up, people told me I wasn't really deaf.

"You can talk, so you can't be deaf."
"You wear hearing aids? Then you're not deaf — you're hard of hearing."
"You can't be deaf if you can hear that."
"You've got selective hearing."
"You're just not paying attention."

And the hardest part?
I started believing them.

I went to a mainstream school. No one else had hearing loss.
My family didn't really talk about it.

There were no deaf role models around me.
I felt… invisible.

I taught myself to lipread just so I could keep up.
But it came at a cost.

I started masking, hiding how much effort it took just to follow a conversation.
Pretending everything was fine when, inside, I was exhausted, anxious, and ashamed.

My hearing loss was mostly in the high-frequency range, which meant I could hear a car engine idling outside —
but not the person speaking next to me.

People didn't understand.
They just saw a girl who "wasn't trying hard enough."

They called me lazy.
Ignored me.
Told me I was rude.
Said I wasn't paying attention.
Told me to "try harder."

At school, a lady used to come in to test my hearing and give me speech tasks.

She was cold. I didn't feel safe asking questions.
It felt clinical, not supportive.
Like I was a checklist to be managed.
Like I was a problem to be solved.

At home, it wasn't much different.
My family didn't empower me — they felt
sorry for me.
And when people feel sorry for you instead of
seeing your strength, you start to shrink.

That kind of energy… it's heavy for a child to carry.

So I hid my hearing aids.
Stopped wearing them.
Got bullied.
And somewhere along the way…
I began to believe that my deafness was
something to hide.
Something to apologise for.
Something to be ashamed of.

But the truth is, it never was.

Reflective prompt

- What things have people said about you that made you question yourself?

- Have you ever hidden a part of who you are, just to feel accepted?

- If someone said those things to your younger self today, what would you want to say back?

Space for reflection

Chapter Four

WHEN THE WORLD GOT QUIETER

I wasn't born deaf.

I lost my hearing when I was around four years old.

It started after I caught a bad case of mumps. After that, it was illness after illness — ear infections, tonsillitis, vomiting episodes that nobody could explain.
My family called me a "sickly kid."
And I guess I was.

I remember being in and out of hospitals.
I remember the way loud sounds made me cover my ears.
I remember my mum telling me off when I didn't respond.
And I remember feeling confused — because I didn't know anything was wrong.
To me, that was just… life.

It wasn't until I was around eight or nine years old that someone really noticed.

I went into hospital to have my tonsils removed and grommets put in.
After the surgery, the consultant turned to my mum and asked:

"Have you ever known Kerry to struggle with hearing?"

My mum told him, "Yes… her friends say 'bye' and she ignores them. She has the TV really loud. I'm always telling her off for being ignorant."

That moment changed everything.

The doctor told my mum my ears were damaged.
The mumps had left a mark.
They couldn't even fit the grommets.
I had severe hearing loss.

And I remember what followed:
Test after test.

And then, my first hearing aids.
Right before starting high school.

But what I remember more than anything…
was how unhappy I felt.
Not just because of the hearing loss — but because for so long, I had been blamed for something I didn't even know was happening.

I'd been told off.
Misunderstood.
Called lazy. Ignorant. Difficult. Disobedient.
When really, I was just deaf.

Every time someone told me my hearing had worsened, it felt like I lost another piece of myself. It wasn't just my ears, it was my confidence, my trust, my joy.

Now, as an adult, I look back on that little girl — and I just want to hug her.

She didn't deserve to be shamed.
She deserved support, love, and someone to tell her it wasn't her fault.

Reflective prompt

- What would you say to your younger self right now if you could go back?

- Has anyone ever misunderstood you because of something invisible — like your hearing, your mental health, or your identity?

- Do you carry any old labels or stories that no longer belong to you?

Space for reflection

Chapter Five

THE FOSTER KID & THE DEAF KID

Home wasn't an easy place for me.

My mum did the best she could, but she had her own struggles.
My dad wasn't in my life at that point.
I had two younger siblings, and I often felt caught in the middle — unseen, unheard.

To be honest, a lot of my memories from that time are cloudy.

That's what trauma can do — it wraps some moments in fog, as a way of protecting us.

I remember being in high school when things finally broke down.

The relationship with my mum became too difficult, and I was placed in foster care.

I was scared.
Lonely.
And I had no idea what the future held.

Even though I was the one being moved around,
I didn't get a say in most decisions.
Social workers, foster carers, even my mum still had more power over my life than I did.

I felt silenced.
I felt small.
And I began to struggle with my mental health.

There were kind moments, too, like the way my best friend's family welcomed me in.
They'd invite me to dinner and treat me like one of their own.
Those moments gave me something I didn't know I was starving for: a feeling of belonging.

But even with that love, I still felt split in two.

I was "the foster kid".
I was "the deaf kid".
And I didn't want to be either.
I just wanted to be Kerry.

I stopped wearing my hearing aids.
At one point, they even went through the wash in my school blazer — and I didn't care.
To me, they were a symbol of everything that made me different.

And I was so tired of being different.

I craved what so many of us crave when we're young:
A "normal" life.
A family that felt safe.
Ears that didn't make me feel broken.
A life where I didn't have to hide parts of myself just to survive.

Reflective prompt

- Have you ever felt like your identity was chosen for you — by your family, by school, or by your circumstances?

- What parts of yourself have you tried to hide to feel "normal"?

- If you could describe the version of "you" that just wants to feel safe, what would it look or sound like?

Space for reflection

Chapter Six

THE SILENCE GOT LOUDER

When the world shut down in lockdown, so did I.

Masks made lipreading impossible.
Phone calls became terrifying.
And the everyday tasks that most people could do without thinking — like booking a doctor's appointment or sorting out a car MOT — felt like climbing a mountain I didn't have the strength for.

I lost my independence.

And instead of support, I got sighs.
My family would groan when I asked for help making phone calls.
They were impatient. Frustrated.
Like I was a burden.

But I wasn't asking for fun.
I was asking because I *couldn't* hear.
Because I needed help.

Every time I reached out and was met
with frustration, I felt myself shrink a little more.

The anxiety crept in.
The panic attacks became a regular thing.
I stopped going out.
I stopped trying.
And on top of that, I was being discriminated
against at work,
something that shook me so badly, I started losing
my hair and became physically unwell.

My body was carrying it all.
The silence. The shame. The fear of never being
understood.

Even the professionals didn't get it.
I remember breaking down at an audiology
appointment, completely overwhelmed.
And the audiologist looked at me and said:

"You're being overdramatic. It's not like you have
cancer or anything."

That moment hit hard.
Because once again, I was being told that
my experience didn't count.
That I was making it up.
That it wasn't "bad enough" to matter.

But it **did** matter.

And I know now that emotional pain, isolation, and
losing your independence is real harm.

You don't have to be dying for your struggle to matter.

Reflective prompt

- Have you ever been told you were "too much" or "overreacting" when you were just struggling?

- What does support look like to you? Who in your life truly listens and makes you feel safe?

- If you could speak to someone in the future going through what you went through in lockdown, what would you want them to know?

Space for reflection

Chapter Seven

THE DAY HOPE WALKED IN

After everything I'd been through — lockdown, discrimination, shame, silence —
I started to wonder if things would ever change.
If I would ever stop feeling stuck.
Invisible. Small.

But here's the truth:

Long before anything changed on the outside, things were already shifting inside.

I was in therapy.
I was journaling daily.
I was training to become a counsellor, and that meant doing a lot of self-discovery work.

It was during that training that I first heard the term *introjected values,* the idea that we absorb other people's beliefs and carry them as if they were our own.

I realised how much of my identity had been shaped by what the world told me I could or couldn't be.

I had internalised so many false ideas about what it meant to be deaf, to be worthy, to be "enough".

And through therapy, reflection, and coaching…
I started to untangle myself from all of that.

I was healing. Not just physically, but emotionally.
I was starting to find my own voice.
To listen to my needs.
To take off the mask.

And *then* —
one day, my dad took me to see a private audiologist.

I wasn't expecting much.
Honestly, I was scared to hope.
Frustrated, too. Why hadn't anyone suggested this sooner?

But that appointment planted a seed.
The audiologist started talking about something I'd barely heard of before:
A cochlear implant.

I had a million questions.
Would it work?
Would I qualify?
Would I lose the hearing I had left?
Would I even *feel* like me afterward?

But underneath all the questions, something gentle began to rise in me:

Hope.

Not just because of the technology
but because I was finally in a space where people were listening.
Because I had already done the work to believe I was worth the help.
Because I had been building the emotional muscles to hold onto hope, even when it felt fragile.

Hope for more independence.
Hope for less daily struggle.
Hope that maybe, just maybe… I didn't have to carry it all alone anymore.

There were scans. Tests. Endless appointments.

And then came the moment I'll never forget:

I met my consultant surgeon.
He said I qualified.
He handed me the paperwork.

And I signed.

It was official.
I was going to have a cochlear implant.

After that, I dived into learning.
I followed people online.
Watched switch-on stories.

Listened to others who'd walked the path before me.

But something was different this time:
I wasn't just gathering information —
I was connecting.

With them.
With myself.
With the version of me that had been slowly rising from underneath all the noise.

The implant didn't create that version of me.
But it did meet me where I already was:
Ready.
Willing.
Hopeful.

For the first time in a long time,
I believed something good was coming.

Reflective prompt

- When was the last time you felt real hope? What did it feel like in your body?

- What's something you'd love to believe is possible for you, even if it feels far away?

- What helps you feel less alone when you're facing something scary or new?

Space for reflection

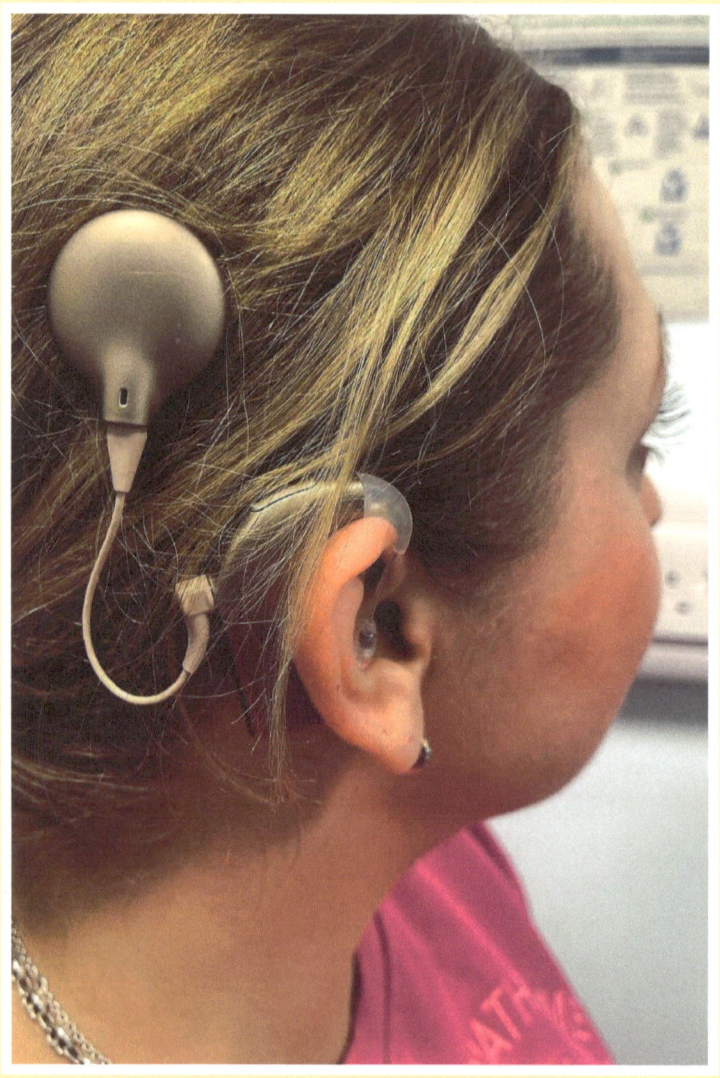

The day of my switch-on

Chapter Eight

STEPPING INTO SOUND

Once I signed the paperwork, the countdown began.
And so did the fear.

What if it didn't work?
What if I didn't wake up?
What if it made things worse?

There were nights I lay awake wondering if I was making the right decision.
But every time the doubt crept in, I reminded myself:
How much worse could it get?

I had already lost so much.
My hearing aids no longer worked.
My world had already gone quiet.
This was my chance to step into a new chapter — and meet the version of me that I had always been meant to become.

The day of my surgery came.
I checked into the ward.
I brought my book, my journal.
I wrote down how I felt — scared, hopeful, nervous, proud.

I had been journaling my whole cochlear implant journey, and reading back reminded me just how far I'd come.

The surgical team were amazing. They made me laugh when I was shaking with nerves.
I felt safe.

I woke up groggy and sick (as I usually am after anaesthetic), but the surgeon told me the surgery had gone really well.
I stayed in hospital a few days to recover — and then, it was just a matter of waiting.

And then came the switch-on.

It happened over two days, and I was equal parts terrified and excited.

On Day One, I started hearing strange squeaky, robotic sounds — like Mickey Mouse playing a broken piano.

It was weird. Funny. Surreal.
I was exhausted by the end of it.

But Day Two?
That's when the magic happened.

That evening, I heard my dog's nails on the floor.
The TV remote made a clicking sound.
There was rain tapping on the window.
And my brain was working overtime — trying to catch up, trying to make sense of it all.

I kept turning to my family:
"What was that?"
"Did you hear that too?"

They'd laugh and say:
"It's the kettle."
"It's the washing machine."

And every sound was like a gift I never knew I'd missed.

I felt proud.
Emotional.
Alive.

But let me be honest: some days were *really* hard.

There were times I had anxious thoughts, times I felt overwhelmed by all the noise, or frustrated when something still didn't sound quite right.
There were days I didn't feel like doing the rehab exercises or tracking the sounds.
But I kept going — because I knew that healing, like anything else worth having, takes **perseverance.**

I reminded myself:
You get out what you put in.

And that's true not just for hearing rehab — but for everything in life.
Whether it's revising for an exam…
Training for your next martial arts belt…
Learning something new or pushing through a hard time…

Perseverance means showing up, even on the hard days.

It doesn't mean being perfect.
It means being consistent.
It means choosing your future self —
over and over again.

I looked back at my journal entries from those first weeks.

> *Week One:*
>
> I heard leaves crunching under my feet…
> The tap was dripping—and it made me laugh, because I once left it on and flooded the kitchen.

> *Week Two:*
>
> I heard birds singing. It's beautiful. I don't remember ever hearing that before.

Day by day, the world opened back up.

> **Week Three:**
> I cried today. Not happy tears —
> frustrated ones.

I was at a café and everything felt *too* loud. The plates clattering, the coffee machine hissing, the background music, people talking all at once, it was overwhelming.

It didn't feel like a gift that day. It felt like chaos. I had to step outside, breathe, and remind myself this was part of the journey.

My brain is still learning. My body is still adjusting. And it's okay to have bad days.

Reflective prompt

- What's a moment in your life where fear and courage existed at the same time?

- What "sounds" or experiences do you want more of in your life — not just literal ones, but emotional ones?

- If you were writing a journal about your journey right now, what would today's entry say?

Space for reflection

Chapter Nine

BELONGING FEELS LIKE THIS

Six months after my surgery, I got an invitation that took my breath away:

Would I like to become a volunteer mentor for the company which made my cochlear implant?

Yes. A thousand times yes!

Choosing a cochlear implant or hearing aid brand is a personal decision.
For me, the one I chose felt just right. I loved the design, the sleek look, the colour options.
It aligned with *me*. With my lifestyle. With my identity.

Some people go bold and bright.
Others choose natural, subtle tones that blend in.
There's no right or wrong.
Just what feels most like you.

Becoming a mentor felt like more than a role.
It felt like purpose.
Like something I had walked through fire to be ready for.

Because suddenly — all the pain, the silence,
the shame — it wasn't just mine to carry anymore.
It could be shared.
Transformed.
Used to help someone else feel less alone.

At my very first mentor event, I met Charlotte.
And we just… clicked.
No explanations needed. No long backstory.
We laughed, swapped journeys, shared
our highs and lows — and now she's my CI bestie.

It was the first time I'd felt that kind of ease.
That kind of *belonging*.

Belonging isn't just about being included.
It's about being understood without needing to shrink or over-explain.
It's about walking into a space and feeling your body relax.
Your shoulders drop.
Your nervous system softens.

It's the ache in your cheeks from smiling too much.
It's knowing you're not "too much" or
"not enough".
You're just *you*. And that's more than enough.

Mentoring gave me a deep sense of fulfilment.

Not because I had all the answers —
but because I could be the person I once needed.
Someone who says:
"You're not alone. You belong here. You don't have to pretend anymore."

But let me be real with you:

Not every space will feel like that.

And that's okay.
Some rooms will make you feel small.
Some circles won't get it.
Some people won't understand your experience —
and they don't have to.
You don't owe them that.

What matters is that you keep looking.
Keep searching for the places where you can be fully yourself.
Find the people who speak your language — even if it's in gestures, expressions, shared silences.
Find your tribe.
They might be deaf. They might be hearing.
Find the ones who see you before you explain yourself.

But most of all? **Find your voice.**

Because even before you find your people — *you* are your first safe space.
And when you start showing up as your whole self, unapologetically,
the right people will find *you* too.

Reflective prompt

- When was the last time you truly felt like you belonged?

- Who in your life makes you feel safe to be fully yourself?

- If you could be a mentor to someone else, what lived experience would you want to share with them?

Space for reflection

Chapter Ten
I AM DEAF — AND I AM FREE

Something changed in me.
Not all at once — but day by day, layer by layer,
I started coming home to myself.

Owning my deaf identity on my terms gave me something I'd never truly had before:
Peace.

I stopped hiding my devices.
In fact — I decorated them with stickers.
I showed them off like jewellery.
I stopped whispering the word "deaf" and started saying it with confidence.

"I'm deaf."

Not a disclaimer.
Not an apology.
Just a fact. A proud, beautiful fact.

I started sharing my story on social media.
Blogging, podcasting and making reels.
Connecting with others in the deaf and hard of hearing community.
I built a whole new network — and found
my people.

I began advocating for myself at work.
Setting boundaries.
Saying no.
Letting go of the version of me who used to stay quiet to stay safe.

I went to cafés. Museums.
Places that used to feel overwhelming.
I travelled on trains.
Drove more.
Spoke on Zoom.
Took up space.

I showed up as my whole self.
My vocabulary changed, too.
I no longer said, "I have a hearing impairment" or "I'm partially deaf."
I said:

"I'm deaf."

And it felt good.
It felt right.
It felt like telling the truth — finally.

I made peace with the parts of me that once felt broken.

And every time I did something that scared me, I whispered to myself:
"Feel the fear — and do it anyway."
And I did.

But here's something I never imagined back then:
Even with access to sound through hearing devices — **some days, I now choose to leave them at home.**

Not because I'm ashamed.
Not because I've given up.
But because I've grown into full acceptance.

Some days, the world is just too loud.
The noise. The energy. The constant stimulation — it's a lot.
And on those days, I choose silence.

I choose stillness.
I choose what's best for me — not what's expected of me.

Hearing devices are not a cure.
They're a support. A tool. A choice.
And I get to decide when and how I use them.

That is freedom.

There was a time I wouldn't have dared to go out without them.
I would've felt unsafe. Uncertain. Worried what others would think.
But now?

I know who I am — with or without sound.
With or without technology.
With or without anyone's permission.

I don't need to hear everything to be confident.
I don't need to "pass for hearing" to feel successful.
I don't need sound to take up space in this world.
Because I've already claimed it — as me.

Fully. Freely. Unapologetically. Deaf.

Reflective prompt

- Which parts of yourself have you been hiding that you're ready to show the world?

- What would your life look like if you stopped apologising for who you are?

- Finish this sentence:
  "I am ____, and I am proud."

Space for reflection

Chapter Eleven

YOU DON'T HAVE TO FOLLOW THEIR RULES

I didn't grow up doing martial arts.
I started later in life — after I'd already been told what I couldn't do too many times.
Too deaf.
Too female.
Too emotional.
Too late.

But when I stepped onto the mat, something in me woke up.

Martial arts didn't just teach me how to fight — they taught me how to *rise*.

They helped me reconnect with my body.
They gave me discipline, strength, awareness — and peace.

They reminded me that I get to move through life in my own rhythm, my own way.

And one of the biggest lessons they taught me?

You can't win a fight playing by someone else's rules.

You can't train to make other people comfortable. You can't grow while trying to fit into a version of you that was written by other people's fears. And you definitely can't reclaim your power by following a script that was never yours.

Life is a lot like martial arts —
especially if you're deaf, disabled, neurodivergent, or different in any way.

From early on, people try to tell us who we're allowed to be.
How to sit. Speak. Learn. Show up.
They write the rules.
And they expect us to play along.

But here's what I've learned — in life, and on the mat:

You don't need to ask permission to be powerful.

People have told me all kinds of things over the years:

"Deaf people can't drive."
"Deaf people can't teach martial arts."
"Deaf people can't live independent lives."
"Deaf people can't be therapists."
"Deaf people can't thrive."

And yet — here I am.
Driving. Teaching. Healing. Coaching. Living. Thriving.
Unapologetically.

I'm not an exception.
I'm proof that the rules were never made for us in the first place.

People fear what they don't understand.
And when they haven't claimed their own power, they'll try to shrink yours too.

So, when someone tells you:
"You can't do that" —
you don't have to shrink.
You don't have to prove anything.

But if you want to?

Say: "Watch me. And take a picture."

This is what I teach at *The Holistic Dojo* —
that your life is your practice.
Your identity is not a limitation.
It's your strength.

Self-awareness is your superpower.
Self-leadership is your secret weapon.

And your voice? Your truth?
They're what break the cycle.

Just like every superhero, you've got your origin story.

You've lived through the hard chapters. The doubt. The rebuilding.

But here's the plot twist:

You are the author now.

You don't have to follow their rules.
You don't even have to read from their book.
You're writing your own.

And it's already worth reading.

Reflective prompt

- What "rules" have you been told you had to follow — but deep down knew weren't yours?

- If you were writing your story today, what kind of main character would you be?

- What is your superpower — and how are you using it right now?

Space for reflection

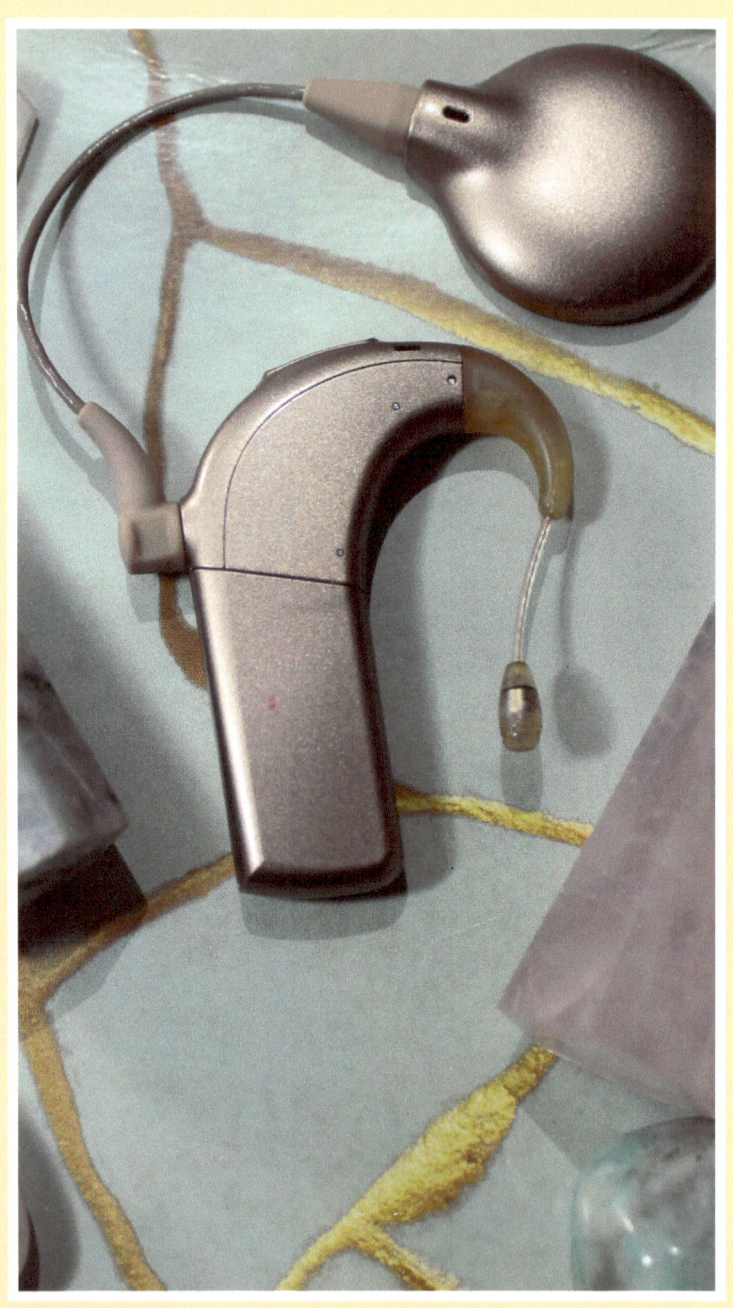

Chapter Twelve

BENEATH THE GOLD

You are not broken.

Read that again.
You are not broken.

For years, I believed I was.
I hid parts of myself like shadows.
I masked. I shrank. I played small.
I let other people's voices become louder
than my own.

But then I found something that changed everything:
Kintsugi.

Kintsugi is a Japanese art form that repairs broken pottery using gold.
Instead of hiding the cracks —
it fills them with beauty.

It says, *This piece isn't ruined—this piece is whole. Stronger. Wiser. More valuable because of what it's been through.*

When I discovered *Kintsugi*, I finally understood something:
My deafness wasn't a flaw.
My trauma wasn't something to be ashamed of.
Every crack in my story was a place where the light could get in — and where the gold could shine.

I started doing something called **shadow work** — learning to face the parts of me I had pushed away.
The insecure parts.
The scared parts.
The ones that just wanted to be seen.

And the moment I brought those parts
into the light?
I felt something I hadn't felt in a long time:
Self-acceptance.

It is never too late.
Never too late to start journaling.
Never too late to speak your truth.
Never too late to come home to yourself.

If you're struggling with your confidence, your mental health, your identity, or your place in the world — I want you to know:

I hear you.
I see you.
I *was* you.

And I promise, things can get better.
Not overnight.
Not all at once.
But slowly, beautifully, with time, truth, and gold.

There's a concept in Japan called **Ikigai.**
It means your reason for being.
Your purpose.
The thing that makes you want to get up each morning.

You have an *Ikigai*.
Even if you don't know it yet.
Even if it's hiding under grief, fear, or confusion.

You were never meant to be like everyone else.

You were meant to be **you.**

So, stop playing small.
Stop waiting for someone else to give you permission.
You are the author now.
You hold the pen.

Discover who you are beneath the noise.
Discover who you are beneath the shame.
Discover who you are… **beneath the gold**.

Reflective prompt

- What cracks in your story are ready to be filled with gold?

- If you were to name your *Ikigai* — your reason for being — what might it be?

- Who are you becoming now that you've stopped hiding?

Space for reflection

Presenting "How Do You Deaf?" at TEDx Wolverhampton. A younger version of me would never have imagined this possible, not even in my wildest dreams... but here I am, doing it.

Chapter Thirteen

SO... HOW DO YOU DEAF?

I've asked myself this question more times than I can count:
So... how do you deaf?

Not in the way other people might expect.
Not with charts or speech scores or audiology reports.
But deep down — in the quiet spaces —
I've asked:

What does being deaf mean to me?

And the truth is... that answer has changed.
Over time. With growth. With healing.
And it might keep changing. That's okay.

Some of us wear hearing aids.
Some of us have cochlear implants.
Some of us use Sign Language.

Some of us speak, some of us don't.
Some of us grew up deaf, some of us became deaf later.
Some of us embrace Deaf culture. Some don't.

And every single version of that is valid.

There is no one right way to be deaf.

Your deafness is not a costume to fit into.
It's not something to measure.
It's not a competition or a checklist.
It's a *part* of who you are — but it doesn't define *all* of who you are.

If I had never been given a cochlear implant…
I would *still* be on a journey of healing and acceptance.
Because the real work wasn't about sound.
It was about self.

Therapy.
Journaling.
Sitting with hard truths.
Finding joy in small things — like the sun through my window, the smell of a candle, the first sip of coffee.
Those are the things that saved me.

And I want you to hear this loud and clear:

Your success is not measured by what's on your ears.

It's measured by your mindset.
Your courage.
Your values.
Your perseverance.
Your self-awareness.
Your truth.

You can be thriving, growing, glowing —
and *still* be deaf.
You don't need tech or speech or hearing levels to validate your worth.

My hearing loss is part of my story.
But it is not the title of my book.

I'm not just a deaf woman.
I'm a grandma. A coach. A therapist. A survivor.
A creative. A warrior.
So many things that don't need labels — just love.

So… how do I deaf?

I do it my way.
With grace. With grit. With gold.
And you get to do it your way, too.

Final prompt

- How do *you* define your deafness or hearing loss?

- What parts of your identity feel most important to you today?

- What's one thing you want the world to understand about your experience?

Space for reflection

ABOUT THE AUTHOR

I'm Kerry — a deaf woman, therapist, school counsellor, founder of *The Holistic Dojo*, martial artist, mum, grandma, and someone who knows what it feels like to carry silence like a second skin.

I've worked as a school counsellor for many years, supporting young people with their identity, emotions, and mental health. I have a background in the National Health Service and bring a holistic, trauma-informed approach to everything I do. I'm also a proud mum to a neurodivergent child — so I understand the real-life challenges of navigating systems, advocating for your needs, and staying connected to who you are.

I created *The Holistic Dojo* to offer a safe space for people to explore who they are — beyond the labels, beyond the noise. It's a space rooted in identity, healing, and self-leadership, blending eastern wisdom, therapeutic tools, and lived experience. It's where people are reminded: you are not broken — you are gold.

I have a cochlear implant now. It's given me access to sound, yes — but more than that, it's given me back my voice. It's reminded me that identity isn't about labels — it's about wholeness.

That healing isn't about going backwards — it's about coming home to yourself.

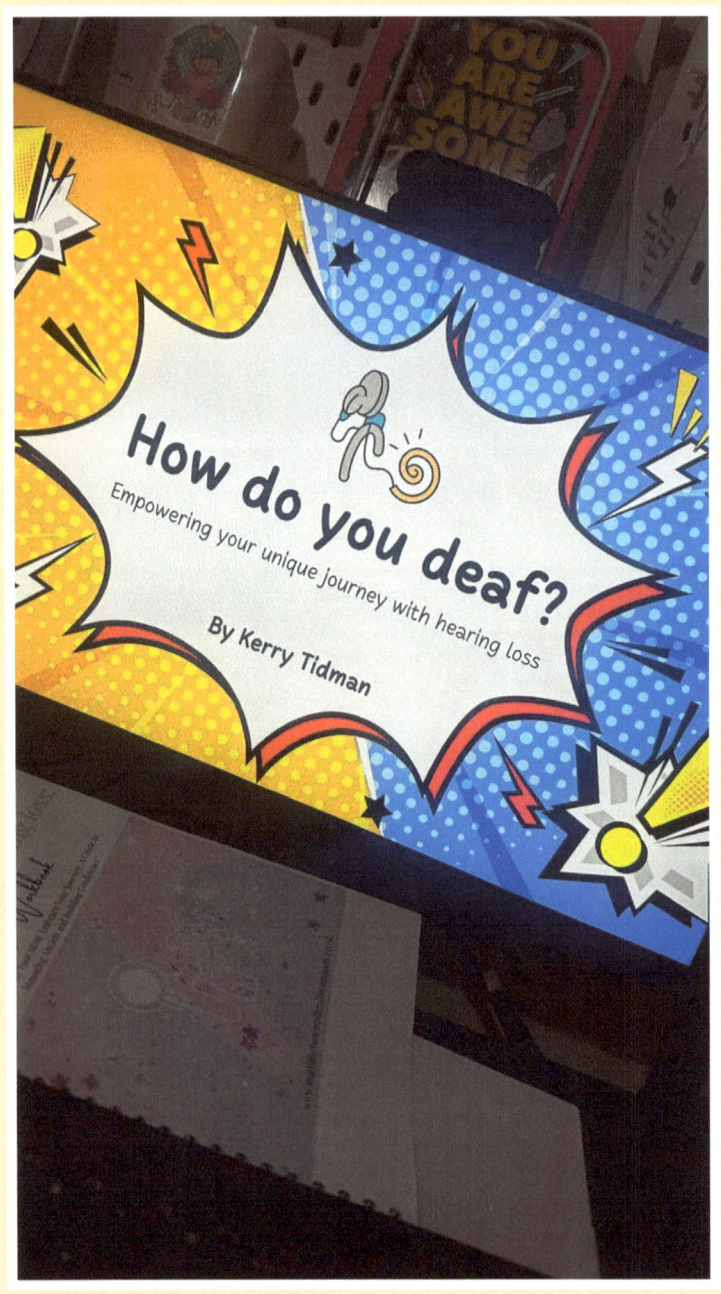

I now share my journey through *Deafinitely Her* — a podcast all about Hearing, Empowerment, and Resilience, where I speak openly about deaf identity, mental health, workplace barriers, self-worth, and everything in between. I also blog on Instagram as *Deafinitely Kerry*, where I raise awareness, share real stories, and show what life is really like as a deaf woman in a hearing world.

This book is the first in a series I've created to help young people like you reconnect with your truth, embrace your deaf identity, and build a more loving relationship with yourself.

Like the Japanese art of *Kintsugi* — where cracks are filled with gold — this book is a reminder that your story doesn't need to be perfect to be powerful.

You are worthy just as you are.
You get to take up space.
You are not alone.
And I am so, so proud of you for being here.

Kerry xx

You're welcome to join me in any of these safe spaces:

Instagram: @deafinitelykerry

Podcast: @DEAFinitelyHER

The Holistic Dojo:
www.theholisticdojo.co.uk

More books from

AVID LANGUAGE

Inclusive books for families with (and without) hearing loss

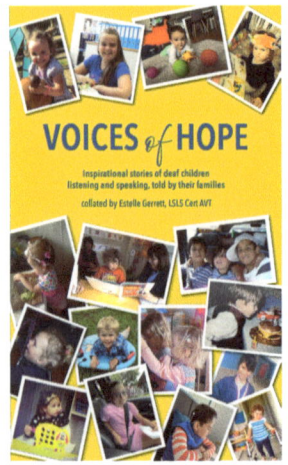

View our full range at **avidlanguage.com**

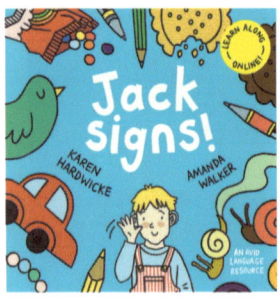
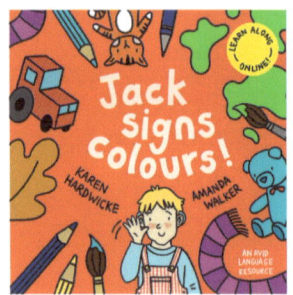
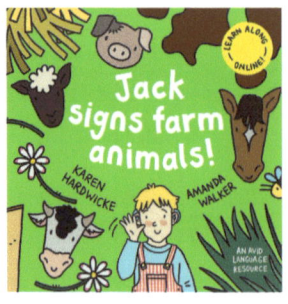

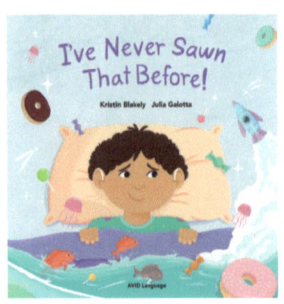
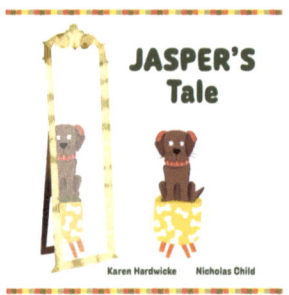

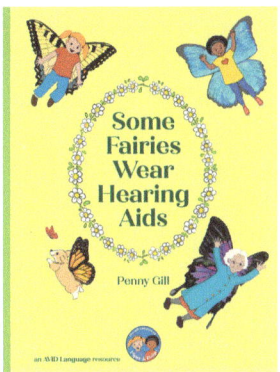
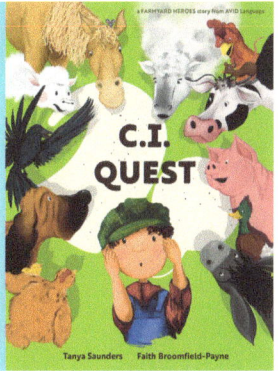

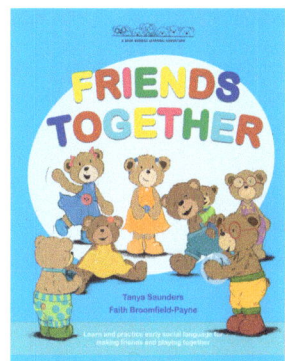
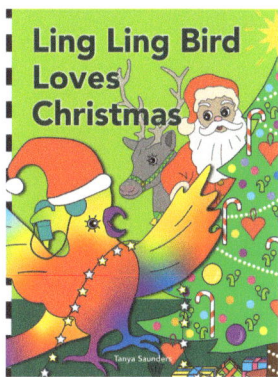

We offer books in multiple languages:

Important

DISCLAIMERS

This book is designed to provide general guidance and to support confidence-building for individuals who are deaf or hard of hearing. It is not a substitute for professional medical advice, diagnosis, or intervention. Always seek the advice of your physician, audiologist, or qualified mental health professional with any questions you may have regarding a medical condition or mental health concerns. The reflection prompts throughout the book are intended to complement professional care and are based on personal experience and general wellness principles. Individual results may vary. Neither the author nor the publisher are liable for any actions taken by individuals based on or in response to the contents of this book.

HOW DO YOU DEAF?
Published by Avid Language Ltd, 3 Cam Drive, Ely, CB6 2WH, UK
First published in 2025

ISBN
Paperback: 978-1-913968-93-9
Hardcover: 978-1-913968-94-6

Text © Kerry Tidman 2025
All photographs © Kerry Tidman 2025, except for
Pages 4, 6, 14, 20, 38, 48, 72, 90 photographs © Daniella Arenare 2025
Page 26 photograph © Sala Saunders 2025
Page 90 photograph © Anna-Mhairi Kane 2025

Editing & Design by Tanya Saunders for AVID Language Ltd.

All rights reserved.

 Inclusive books for families with (and without) hearing loss

www.avidlanguage.com

www.ingramcontent.com/pod-product-compliance
Lightning Source LLC
Chambersburg PA
CBHW041219070526
44584CB00001B/17